Niyara presents:

Nandita Chatterjee &
Reena Patel

Copyright © Nandita Chatterjee 2023
All Rights Reserved.

ISBN 979-8-89026-690-3

This book has been published with all efforts taken to make the material error-free after the consent of the author. However, the author and the publisher do not assume and hereby disclaim any liability to any party for any loss, damage, or disruption caused by errors or omissions, whether such errors or omissions result from negligence, accident, or any other cause.

While every effort has been made to avoid any mistake or omission, this publication is being sold on the condition and understanding that neither the author nor the publishers or printers would be liable in any manner to any person by reason of any mistake or omission in this publication or for any action taken or omitted to be taken or advice rendered or accepted on the basis of this work. For any defect in printing or binding the publishers will be liable only to replace the defective copy by another copy of this work then available.

Dedication

For Niyara Lily Varma & her Dodo Ms. Nelly Chatterjee; teacher & grandmother that inspired soo many of her students to achieve their dreams and today is a pillar of support and unconditional love to her granddaughter.

Your love for each other is unmatched and infinite

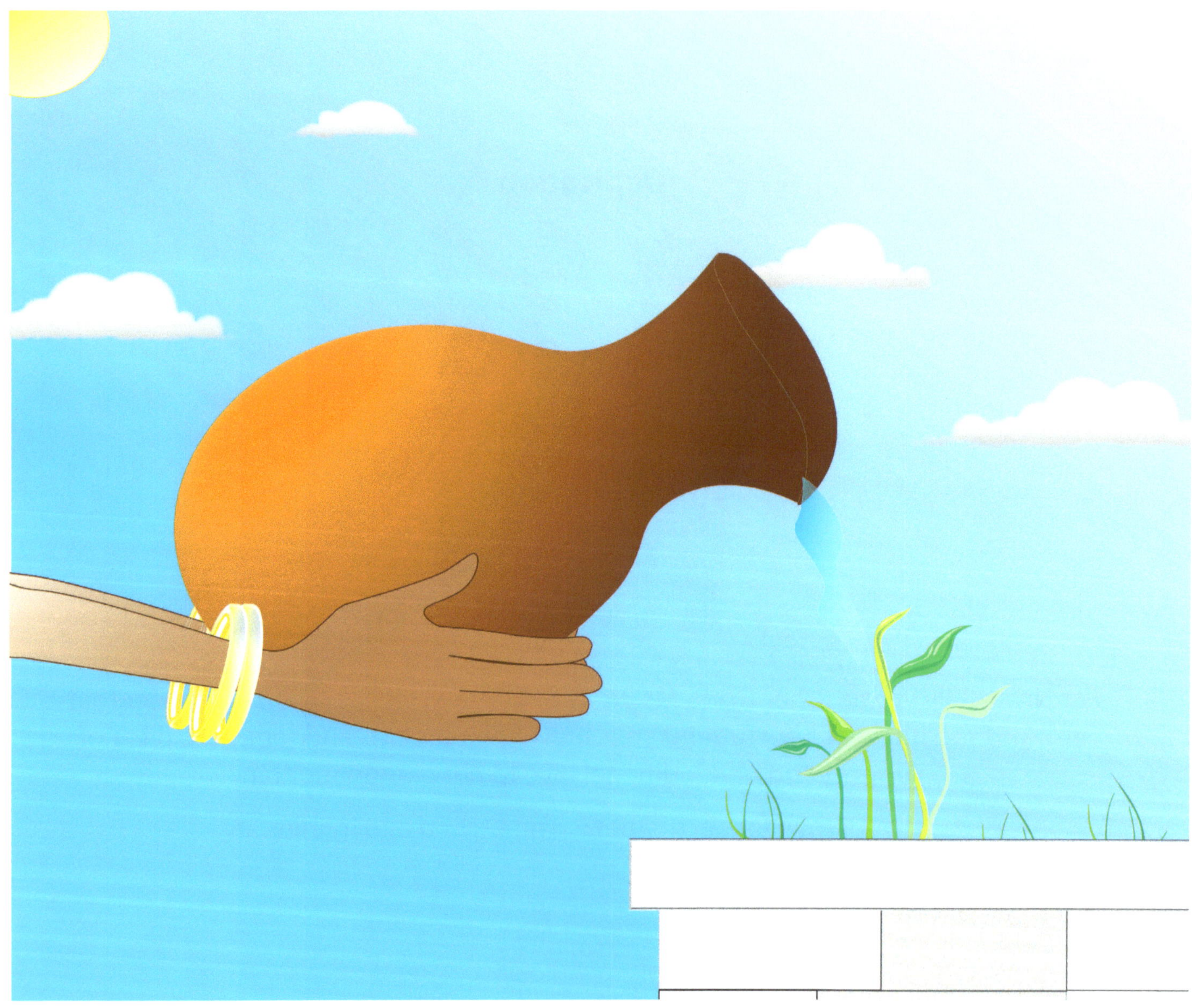

It's Six A.M. and the sun is on the rise.
Outside Asha's window, she sees her Ba holding her magical brass pot pouring water in the direction of the sun.

Asha knows it's special blessings she seeks from the power of the bright rays of the sun so that her home and family may be filled with warmth.

“Wake up my jaan!”, Asha’s mother nudges Asha awake.
“It’s a special day today. Asha’s first day of school!”

Asha jumps up knowing that this is the first time she will be away from home all day! A great day filled with new friends and play.
She rushed to get ready and look her best to show the world she is ready for what adventures come next.

Her hair tied in a tight braid with colorful ends her aunt sent her from india in bright hues of pink and orange.

On her wrist, she wore shiney bangles with glitter and sparkle. She bought them herself, over the summer, when they went to India for her cousin’s wedding.

As a breakfast for champs, Ba made her favorite breakfast, Dosa. Asha loved eating Dosa for its crunchy crepe-like texture and delicious filling made of spicy potatoes.

Asha looked out the window and saw a bright yellow bus not too far away. She rushed to put on her shoes as her mother helped her put on her backpack.

But before Asha opened the door, Ba fed her a spoon of sweet yogurt for good luck. Asha touched Ba's feet to seek her blessings for the new adventure waiting for her outside her door. She was ready to embark on her yellow chariot.

As Asha hopped off of the chariot, she ran onto the blacktop with the other children to find her line. She had checked the class list with her dad over the weekend to find out who her teacher was.

"Mrs. Mortan's first grade line!", called out a young woman with red hair, freckles, and a smile so kind and so beautiful.

Asha got in line and waited for her name to be called.

"Asha Patel!", Mrs. Mortan called.

"Here!", Asha excitedly yelled as she ran to the front of the line.

In her excitement, she didn't notice Chris Radwin, a second grader and the meanest bully in school, snickering at her and laughing with his friends. "Ashes? Her name is Ashes!", he hollered and laughed.

It took Asha a while to notice that he was talking about her. She was sad but wasn't going to let that stop her.

As the clock struck 12, all the students were ushered to the lunch room.

Asha was excited as this was when she would actually get to make some friends.

She sat next a few girls from her class who were giving her an odd stare.

"What's that in your hair?", asked Kim. "It looks like gum balls." All the girls started laughing at Asha's braided hair.

Asha was wearing a paranda, an Indian style beret made of glass.

With her head down, Asha opened her lunch box to eat the Theplas, a flat bread made with mint and spinach, that Ba had packed her.

The other girls stared as she ate and whispered amongst eachother.

Three VERY LONG Hours went by. It was time to go home and Asha was relieved. She grabbed her backpack and headed to her bus. She didn't realize that Chris and his friends were standing in line behind her waiting for the same bus.

The whole way home they sang, "Ashes, Ashes we all fall down!".

As soon as Asha got home, she ran to her Ba.

Crying her eyes out as she decided she wouldn't go back to school.

Her Ba heard her out but told Asha that she had an idea.

The next day Ba decided to accompany Asha to school and have a little talk with her teacher.

As Ba was leaving, Asha felt a pang in her stomach.

Right before lunch, Mrs. Mortan made an announcement.

"We have Mrs. Patel here today and she would like to share something with you."

Standing, was Ba dressed in a top and a beautiful skirt, instead of a sari.

Asha had forgotten that long ago Ba was a teacher, just like Mrs. Mortan.

"I am Mrs. Patel and I would like to introduce you to my granddaughter, Asha.", Ba said as she smiled at Asha.

"For starters, I would like to tell you that her name means 'hope'. We named her that because the day she was born, our family got new hope for a bigger, brighter future. Asha's dad, who is a scientist, suddenly got an approval for a drug that he was working on for years. This was a drug that would save the lives of many children across the world suffering from leukemia".

Ba went on to share pictures of where her ancestors came from.

She described a land full of colors and flavors.

At the end of her speech, Ba brought out a giant bag of samosas filled with vegetarian pizza stuffing and passed it around.

All the kids loved the taste and demanded more.

She also brought out a bag of shiny glass bangles, wrapped in fours, and said, "This is a gift from Asha for her new friends! Who here is her friend?"

Kim, the girl who made fun of Asha yesterday, was the first one to make a bee line followed by the rest.

Ba smiled at Mrs. Mortan and Asha as Asha's new friends fled to her.

They were excited and were asking Asha so many questions about her family, culture, and food.

They wanted to know more!

Asha was so surprised that she didn't realize that her future was going to take a turn for the better.

Ever since, Asha's classmates would race to sit next to her at lunch and Chris and Kim were regulars at the Patels for Ba's samosas and play dates.

What Ba taught Asha and her friends that day, is that people are sometimes afraid of the unknown.

To protect themselves, they make fun of things that are new and unknown or uncomfortable.

It is up to you to share your story and show others the magic in discovering new things and seeing how each person's story can teach you about life.

www.ingramcontent.com/pod-product-compliance
Lightning Source LLC
LaVergne TN
LVHW071134160826
845679LV00005B/1285

9798890266903